The Ghost Det

Ghost Detective I: ISBN 978-0-9532563-3-4

Ghost Detective II: ISBN 978-0-9532563-4-1

Ghost Detective III: ISBN 978-0-9532563-5-8

Ghost Detective IV: ISBN 978-0-9532563-7-2

Ghost Detective V: ISBN 978-0-9532563-8-9

Ghost Detective VI: ISBN 978-0-9532563-9-6

www.ghost-detective.com

©Adrian Perkins 2019

The right of Adrian Perkins to be identified as the author of this work has been asserted in accordance with the Copyrights, Design and Patent Act. 1988.

All rights reserved. No part of this book may be reprinted or reproduced or utilised in any form or by any electronic mechanical or other means, now known or invented, including photocopying and recording, or in any information storage or retrieval system, without the written permission from the author.

British Library Cataloguing in Publication Data. A catalogue record for this series of books is available from the British Library.

Contents

Eyewitness stories from Passenham Village, Milton Keynes, England

Investigation into ghosts at Gray's Roade House Hotel, Northamptonshire, England

Eyewitness account of time slip at the Llansantffraed Court hotel, Abergavenny, Wales

Eyewitness account of the ghosts in Hazelwood Roade, Bedfordshire, England

Eyewitness account of the hitchhiker of Stranraer, Inch, Dumfries and Galloway, southwest Scotland

Investigation of the ghosts at the S Bar in Stilton, Cambridgeshire, England

Eyewitness account of friendly ghosts in Higham Ferrers, East Northamptonshire, England

Eyewitness account of the ghost cat from Lancashire, England

Eyewitness account of the friendly ghost of Mary in Peterborough, Cambridgeshire, England.

Investigation of the dormouse of Deanshanger, Milton Keynes, England

Eyewitness account of the ghosts of Hawkers Cottage, Cornwall, England

Eyewitness account of ghosts that haunt the former Royal Ordnance Depot at Weedon Bec in Northamptonshire, England

Gruesome Story from the railway at Ashton, Northamptonshire, England.

The ten year anniversary investigation at Twinwood Farm in Bedfordshire, England

Acknowledgements

Peter & Vanessa Gray
Gray's Roade House Hotel

Terry & Nathan
The S-Bar in Stilton

All Contributors
For
Eyewitness Stories

Northamptonshire Records Office

Phipps Northampton Brewery Company

Peterborough Images

David Rayner
For the Stilton fire photos

Chris Hillyard
A Baby Cries
From his forthcoming book
A cut above the rest

Book Cover Photos
Lewis Dellar
With kind Permission from
Royal Ordnance Depot, Weedon Bec,
Northamptonshire

4

Ghost Detective
VII

Copyright © A H Perkins

All rights reserved.

Paris & Wolf Publishing

25th May 2019

ISBN 978-0-9955011-0-2

Introduction

My experiences over the years have altered my thinking regarding many aspects of the supernatural. If you seek the truth about this subject you must first remove all mysticism, and religion, and approach it with uncluttered thoughts. When I conduct an investigation, or interview someone about activity they may have seen or experienced, I try to do it without being judgmental. I gather all the information as thoroughly as I can. Later, I will start piecing together the facts and do the necessary research. The people I help understandably want answers after I have completed the investigation. It doesn't surprise me if they reject my findings. Clients always form their own conclusions long before I come on the scene. Occasionally you do get the open-minded person who reads your research, and it gives them the answers they were looking for. For me that is a result. If I can set the seed of interest in someone's mind that sends them onto their own journey of discovery, then I'm a happy man.

This book took longer to compile than I had anticipated and many of the stories I investigated didn't make the page, simply because they were not strong enough. But I hope you will like the stories and investigations that did. While writing I am always trying to give the reader as much information as possible. I want you to be able to visit the locations, and with the story in mind, get a feel for the energy that is still there. I have a theory about ghosts and spirits that has been formed over many years of research. If I explain it now it may help you understand some aspects of the following investigations and stories.

A ghost is a recording of an event that has happened to a person or an animal. The recording is so detailed when it's first made you would find it hard to tell it from a living being. It's not just the image that's recorded; sound and smell might also be recorded. The only thing that sets it apart from the living is it's no longer physical, and can't interact with our physical world. Only a spirit can do that. Over the centuries the ghost recording starts to deteriorate. The first thing to go is colour, and then it becomes semi-transparent. After that, part of the image will go, and then all of it will disappear leaving just sound and smell. The last things to go from a ghost recording are smells, like tobacco or scent. Have you ever sat in your house and smelt tobacco, or a strong scent? So why and how is a recording made. I believe recordings are made because the dying person or animal is suddenly shocked at the point of death. This sudden emotional shock releases an energy from us that is so strong it is fixed in the atmosphere where the event took place. Events like suicide, murder, road accident, indeed anything that takes life suddenly.

When I talk about spirit, this is not in the spiritual sense. I call the inner person the spirit, the part of you that creates your imagination, and what makes you who you are and guides your life. Just for a moment forget mysticism and religion, and think of yourself as an operating individual, within a biological shell. When your body dies your spirit is released from the body and takes on a different form. It's conscious of its surroundings and the people around it. I have interviewed many people who have had near death experiences. They all tell the same tale of being outside their body looking back at themselves and at the people around them. They also say they are without pain, and feel an overwhelming sense of peace. As we live our physical lives we deteriorate. Our bodies grow old and we suffer pain from our joints and other physical problems. Imagine suddenly having that taken away. You would indeed feel an overwhelming sense of peace. I am convinced that we go on after death. I'm not a religious man. I simply have a faith in the living being continuing long after their body dies. Don't get me wrong. Everyone has the right to believe whatever they want to. As long as it doesn't hurt anyone else and it gets you through your life then it's your choice and nobody can take that away from you.

Just remember this. The next time you are looking for help or guidance from a loved one who has died, listen to that little voice in the back of your mind and don't ignore that gut feeling, it's usually the right answer.

Now, sit back, relax, and enjoy the world of ghosts and spirits.
Adrian Perkins

Stories from Passenham

This first eyewitness account is from an old friend Tom Inwood. Our paths cross from time to time, and on this occasion he had time to relate stories from his youth. We are kindred spirits when it comes to ghosts and spirits, and these tales explain why.

Tom lived in Stony Stratford, which is now part of Milton Keynes, from the age of six to twenty-two. In his early teens he used to walk around the streets of Stony, with little to do and nowhere to go. One summer evening he and fifteen others decided to walk to Passenham, a small village in the civil parish of Old Stratford in South Northamptonshire. It is just north of the River Great Ouse, which forms the boundary with Buckinghamshire. They arrived outside the church and stood chatting with each other. Percy Black, a friend of Tom burst out of the church with his girlfriend Rose. She lived in Rose Cottage, next door to the church. They came running down the path shouting, we have just seen a ghost. Their shouts fell on unbelieving ears, but the two insisted that while in the church they had seen a ghost. All fifteen boys decided to see for themselves. Off they went into the church all brave and heroic, not expecting to see anything. They all sat down, taking up both back pews. To get to the pews you go through the main door, through a passageway, under the balcony, through a green curtain, and you are then in the church. They all sat there waiting for something to happen. Tom felt coldness on the back of his neck. Percy then said, "Look up at the balcony it's there again." Tom went through what they saw. Through the door to the side of the balcony appeared what Tom described as flickering stars, which appeared to have a mist following them.

The stars glided along the back wall, down the side wall, back across the front of the balcony and disappeared into the wall by the door. The boys tried to come to a logical answer to what they had all witnessed, and agreed on car lights. Just to prove it they asked Kimmy, one of the boys, to go and sit on a window ledge just by the balcony. It was a summer's day so Kimmy could check if cars that drove by were creating the stars with their headlights.

Tom said, "But it's a summer day, there wouldn't be any headlights." They all felt that coldness on their necks again. Pat Burns was sitting next to Tom, they were mates and nothing usually fazed them. But right at that moment Pat was looking at Tom and looking really scared. As before, the stars appeared and followed the same route. There was a sudden realization from Kimmy that the stars were heading straight for him. With a clatter and bang Kimmy fell off the window ledge and onto the floor. The stars and mist disappeared as they had done before. Now the boys were really scratching their heads, what could it be? They all agreed the stars resembled candlelight as they flickered. Percy then appeared back in the church saying, he'd been to get his camera. He said when it happens again, he'd take a picture of it. They all sat there. It seemed to Tom that the bravery had all but disappeared, and then it happened again. Through the door came the lights followed by the mist, following the same course as before. Percy took his picture. They all sat there still puzzling about what they were seeing. Then Fred, one of the lads, said, "I don't know about the rest of you but I'm getting the hell out of here." En masse the boys jumped up and made for the green curtain. Now although it was a summer's day, between the heavy green curtain and the church door was a passage and it was pitch black in there. Imagine fifteen boys all trying to get out of the church in a hurry, nobody wanted to be last through that curtain. Tom was in the middle of the group and got carried through the passage, through the crush at the door, and took just four steps along the churchyard path to the gate. The boys were running so fast poor Tom got bounced along in the crush. Outside the churchyard the boys took a breather and looked back at the church. Then one of the lads, Alan, stood looking at the church as if he was in a trance. The lads shouted, "Alan" three times. It wasn't until Tom punched him on the arm that he snapped out of his trance. But he didn't know what had happened. He said he had been looking at the cross of stones set in the wall, and the next thing he knew was Tom punching him. So, do the candles and mist still appear in the church balcony? Who knows? Be interesting to find out though, don't you think?

Tom's next story from Passenham concerns a quite well-known character around those parts. One-night, Tom's friend Dave from Stratford, was leaving his girlfriend's cottage next to Passenham church on his pushbike. He had just emerged out from the little group of trees in front of the cottage and on reaching the road he heard the sound of a horse. Wondering who would be riding a horse at that time of night he stopped and waited to see. Suddenly, he saw a white horse galloping at some speed towards him. It was dragging a man who had his foot caught in the stirrup. Dave had no time to react and the horse and its unfortunate rider went straight through his front wheel. Dave was stunned, and it took him a while to regain his thoughts. Whatever he had just seen went straight through his front wheel as if it wasn't there. Moments later the image vanished into thin air. Intrigued by this story I popped over to Passenham to take a closer look at the place. I had heard the usual ghost stories and one of them rang a bell.

The Northampton Daily Echo dated 19th January 1916 had a story: Robert Banastre, who lived at the old Manor House, broke his neck in the hunting field and his horse dragged his mangled body home. Since his violent death the spirit of Banastre has been said to drive his carriage and pair up to the doors of the Manor House, or to go for a midnight gallop on his faithful mare. Was it Robert Banastre Dave had seen?

The Ghost of Nancy Webb

Here is another story connected to Passenham.

On the anniversary of the annual October Deanshanger feast, a figure of a lady in white bearing a child in her arms is supposed to head to the Passenham Mill race, into which she plunges, her white dress floating on the water. The story goes she had lost her husband in the Crimean War and her new born son died shortly after, her name was Nancy Webb and her continued visits to the graveyard unhinged her, reputedly she threw herself in the Mill Race where her body was mangled by the water wheel.

Whether the story is true or not, you really should visit the church at Passenham. Here is a little information for you. The church of St Guthlac has a late 13th-century tower, the upper part being rebuilt in 1626. The chancel was also built in 1626 by Sir Robert Banastre who died in 1649. Some remarkable furnishings, stalls and misericords, (a ledge projecting from the underside of a hinged seat in a choir stall which, when the seat is turned up, gives support to someone standing) date from 1626. There are original wall paintings which were restored in the 1960s. The church also has some fine old box pews and stained glass. Personally, I love the location. I fished the river many years ago, and the peacefulness of the place is something to be enjoyed. Whether you believe in ghosts or not, it's a beautiful place to visit during the summer months.

Ghosts of Gray's Roade House Hotel

Hotel main entrance above

The adjoining Cafeteria was once The White Hart Inn.

Gray's Roade House Hotel and Cafeteria is situated close to the Cock Inn, in the picturesque village of Roade in Northamptonshire. The investigation came about after a chat I had with my good friends Vanessa and Peter Gray from the Cock Inn. I'm always looking for interesting stories and Peter and Vanessa had a story that really made me sit up and listen.

His family history can be traced back for generations in Roade. Not so long ago his family held the trades of Wheelwrights, Coopers, Undertakers, and Builders in the village. As the years went on the work diminished, and eventually they stopped trading. Sadly their old workshops close to the village green burnt down. Peter and Vanessa are the local publicans at the Cock Inn, and at the time of this investigation they also ran Gray's Hotel and Cafe, just across the road. Vanessa managed the hotel and cafe, and sometimes received odd reports from guests staying either at the hotel, or when visiting the cafe. Just small insignificant things, the odd voice was heard, a baby crying, a fleeting glimpse of a figure in a bedroom, and sometimes footsteps being heard in corridors by the staff when they knew they were alone. I asked if an investigation would be possible. Being a busy hotel, this was not going to be easy. We needed everyone connected with the investigation to be available on a date selected by Vanessa, and at short notice. If the hotel had no guests on a particular evening, we would need to be ready to move. Luckily on the 18th of February 2017 the call came. I put the word out to the people I needed on this case and thankfully they were all free. Yes, it really is this complicated to do a business location.

Before we go into the full investigation, you need to get a clear idea of the layout of the property. During the evening people picked up on things in certain rooms and a floor plan will help you follow us around. On the next two pages you will see a floor plan of the Hotel, and one of how things looked before the alterations. After you have read the full investigation, I will let you know more of the location history.

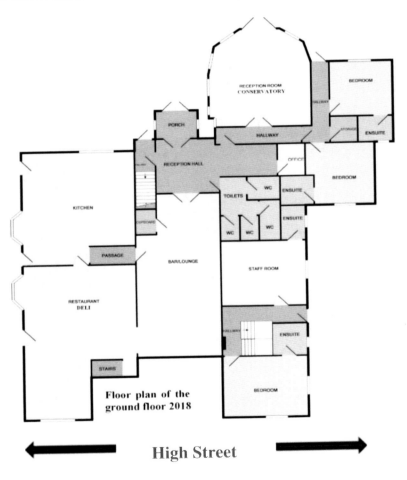

Floor plan of the ground floor 2018

High Street

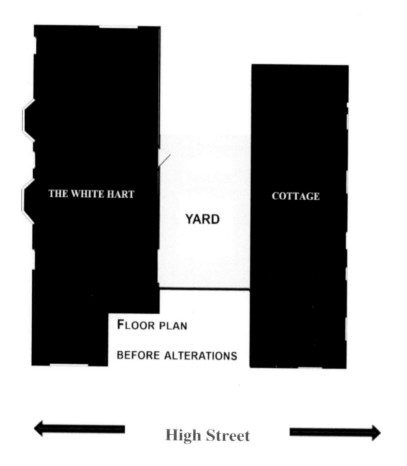

THE WHITE HART

COTTAGE

YARD

FLOOR PLAN

BEFORE ALTERATIONS

← **High Street** →

I wanted this investigation to be totally different, no toys, gadgets, or over the top mediums to lead us down the garden

17

path. This was going to be as natural and unforced as I could get it. I had known the people selected for this case for a while and knew their interests, what's more I knew their potential if given the correct location and investigative technique.

On the case were, Lewis Dellar, Jim and Ann O'Neill, Mark and Emma Whiteman, with Emma's stepdad Denis. Vanessa Gray was observing the proceedings. I'm going to write this down as things happened, so we will be going back and forth between people in the group. It will give you an idea of how spontaneous things happen. We don't stop everything just because one person is getting something; we were there to get as much as possible.

Sitting in the lounge at Grey's

As we began the investigation, in the very comfortable lounge, I wanted everyone as relaxed as possible. My strategy for the case was as I explained before, unforced natural clairvoyance. We started with a light-hearted and good-humoured chat. I then asked Vanessa to turn the lights off, leaving just the one above

18

us on. I asked the group to simply open their mind to the location and say whatever came into their thoughts, whether it made sense to them or not. Lewis got the feeling the place had a connection to Gibraltar, which I would check later. Then Emma Whiteman got a name of Fredrick. I was recording all the time, and what people did not know, was the name Fredrick caused a response, a knocking sound that nobody in the room reacted to, simply because they didn't hear it. Ann O'Neill then felt the presence of a nurse, in front of a group of people, a matron type figure standing in the corner watching the proceedings. Emma saw a man standing in the corner wearing a top hat, slim, and very well dressed with a flower in his black coat lapel. She described him as very prim and proper. Then Jim picked up on the same chap, adding, he had a white collar. Emma said the gentleman said his name was Fredrick. Then Denis said he could see a man in a flat cap which had a little black check pattern on it and he wore a waistcoat with watch chain and fob. The man was walking up and down and held a stick with a silver handle. To Denis it seemed as if the man was waiting for someone or something. The chap then banged his stick on the ground. Emma said she was constantly getting the name Fredrick over and over again. The knock sound came again. Vanessa then said she thought Emma was correct with the name Fredrick, and both she and Denis had the right images. Both of them would now try to concentrate their efforts on these two connections.

Lewis said he could hear a bell toll, the type that announced the death of a person. He could also see a wooden cart going up and down the road. Jim confirmed the image, he could see the same, and it matched what Lewis was describing. Those who could see Fredrick in their mind said he seemed very restless, constantly checking his watch.

All went quiet for a while so I decided we should move to another room to see if the activity would resume. Vanessa decided her husband Peter should hear what was going on so she phoned him and asked him to come over. She then asked if she could tell the group a little of the family history. Vanessa explained that Fredrick Gray was the village undertaker and Peter's grandfather. They used to put coffins on a cart, and as the church bell tolled Fredrick walked in procession with his cane wearing a top hat and long black coat. Vanessa really wanted Peter to be present while all this was happening; however, he was looking after the pub and might have been too busy to join us.

While we waited for Peter, we moved into one of the hotel bedrooms on the ground floor. This in fact had been the living room of a cottage. The cafe part of the property was previously a pub called the White Hart Inn, and the hotel part was formerly the cottage, modernized and extended. As we spread out around the room a Morse code like sound was recorded on the Dictaphone I was using. Remember, all the sounds recorded were only discovered much later while going through the recordings. Vanessa left us to go to get Peter. I think she decided to take over for him, allowing him to join us. As we settled in, I explained we were to follow the same approach as before, relaxed, and natural clairvoyance. Only Vanessa, Peter, Lewis and I knew what this room was used for in the past, so this would be interesting. Ann picked up on an angry confrontation between a man and a woman. She felt as though the male was bullying the female but couldn't determine an age for either one yet. Just then the Dictaphone recorded raised voices, male and female. Emma then said Fredrick had followed them into the room. She got the impression that while we were in the property, he would be with us. I then got the name Pearl. Jim also sensed the presence of a woman in her early twenties. Was this the woman being bullied? Denis was also picking up on a young woman of about the same age in the street on the corner of what was once the pub. She wore a small bonnet and had blond curly hair; she was also wearing a pink dress. Denis got the impression these were her Sunday best clothes. He also sensed she was crying but didn't know why. He could also see a small boy close to her playing with a metal barrel hoop and stick. Now, do you remember what some of the Gray's trades were? Coopers fitted metal bands onto barrels, and wheelwrights fitted metal bands onto wheels, coincidence? Meanwhile Emma was finding it hard to pick up on anything other than Fredrick. It was as though he was blocking any other contact other than with him. This was fine as long as Emma was happy with the situation, which she was. Lewis was sensing there had been an accident and asked if anybody had ever been electrocuted within the building. I would check, but records for this would be hard to locate.

We were still waiting for Peter to come over from the pub and I didn't want to do too much without him. I made the decision not to say anything about the feelings I was picking up, due to the fact I had already interviewed Peter, and knew quite a bit about the rooms we would be going into. I wouldn't know if the feelings were real, or a memory from the interview. We really needed Peter there. I think his presence would boost the contact with Fredrick and Emma.

Back in the room, Lewis came up with a surname of Jacobson, and a date of 1659. This would be easier to check out. Denis then said he saw another building standing in what is now the car park. I know there was once a row of terrace houses standing there. In recent times while cars were parked there after heavy rain, a hole appeared to the side of one of the vehicles. When the row of houses had been pulled down, they forgot to fill in the cellars. So, Denis was correct with what he could see. I still thought the strongest connection so far was between Emma and the spirit Fredrick. He was still with her, but for some reason didn't want to communicate with her in room nine.

We agreed to move into the cafe part of the building, once known as the White Hart public house. I knew Fredrick and the Gray family frequented the pub, I just hoped our visit would bring further information. Just before we left room nine, Ann sensed an angry man banging his fist on a table shouting at her to get out of his room. She got a glimpse of him in her mind's eye and said his face was disfigured from either burning or scalding. She was glad to leave the spirit of the man in his room, and hoped he would not follow her around the hotel as we explored further.

As we walked to the cafe Emma said to me, she was unsure if she liked Fredrick. I think it was his insistence to follow her around that unnerved her. In the cafe we all sat round the same table and gathered our thoughts quietly for a few moments. Remember, apart from Lewis and me, the others knew nothing of the history of the cafe, so I was really interested in what they were going to come up with. I began by asking the spirits around us to come and join us. This part of the building was alive.

After a few minutes of silence Emma began picking up on a young woman called Sarah. She said Sarah seemed to be acting much younger than her years, as if she had developmental problems. She also said Sarah's surname began with either a 'G' or a 'J' and was from the Victorian age. The girl kept repeating, "don't let him hurt me, don't let him hurt me". Emma said the girl was petrified of the spirit who was in the cottage, but now he was in the room with us. Was it Ann's connection? Frustratingly for Ann, she was still having problems with the spirit she connected to as we left the living room of the old cottage. He was still insisting she left the building. She was slightly unnerved by it, but felt she had control. It was plain we had a domineering male, other than Fredrick, one who seemed to enjoy bullying women.

Emma then reported that Fredrick was here, but he was only following what we were doing rather than actively contacting us. If anything, Emma thought he was blocking her in a small way. Peter still had not joined us and I felt this was the reason for Fredrick's distance. Meanwhile, Denis had formed a strong connection to the spirit of an old lady sitting in a rocking chair. She sat crocheting a type of pattern cover, rocking gently back and forth. As she did, she said, "It won't work me dearie, it won't work". Denis said she had a strong accent but he couldn't place it. He also said the spirit said this to him as he mentally tried to put a circle of protection around Ann, to shield her from the unpleasant spirit. Ann did say, for a moment she thought she was looking at us through the unpleasant spirits eyes, and at that moment she felt he was pulled away from her. In past investigations it has been noticed that a large number of spirits in a small location can give their own protection to a person in need of it. Jim and Lewis heard someone enter the building just before we saw Vanessa and Peter walking toward the hotel. At that time Emma saw a shadow walk across the passage that separates the cafe from the bar and lounge.

Now let's see what would happen when Peter and Vanessa joined us. We brought them up to speed with the evening's activity so far. However, before we continued Lewis, our resident parapsychologist, wanted to see if he could recreate the shadow of the person seen moments before Peter and Vanessa walked into the building. He was unable to do it so re-joined us. Peter explained that Fredrick, his grandfather, frequented the White Hart pub, which was the building we were in. Jim had picked up on the bully spirit and had a partial picture of him. He said he was tall and thin, with a beard. Denis could also see him

24

and confirmed Jim's picture, adding, he wore a large hat and cape type raincoat. He said the man was feared more than respected. At that point, and unknown to the group, I recorded the sound of shuffling feet behind Ann, close to where Lewis sat. The recorder I was using was sitting in the middle of the table and also recorded the sound of someone tapping and stroking the microphone.

I asked out again to see if Peter and Vanessa being with us made a difference to the spirit reaction, and it did. After only a few moments we heard a thumping noise close to where we were sitting. Then Peter heard someone singing, I also heard it but further away. Emma felt the need to go and sit in the lounge so she left the group. At this time Denis thought he could hear the singing of Irish songs. He could see two chaps sitting at a table in our room, by the window, having a great time. He then added, a thin tall man then entered the pub and stared at the two chaps in the corner. Someone then said, "Not tonight Mick". Peter said with a chuckle, this pub could tell some tales. I then heard a door slam and Lewis went to investigate, returning moments later saying there was nobody about that could have done that. Emma came back into the room and asked Peter if Fredrick had a heart complaint. Peter said only his father had.
We decided to move back into the lounge to see if this helped. I then asked Peter to actively join in with the circle and was really pleased that he agreed. It's so strange, but when we moved back into the lounge the atmosphere between everyone became light-hearted and jovial. No, we were not drinking, well only tea and coffee.

I sat with Peter listening to what people connected with.

During the years I have known him, Peter shows a real interest in the subject of ghosts and spirits, as does his wife Vanessa. However, there is reluctance in him to delve too deeply. He acknowledges the experiences he has had in the past, but would rather not take the chance of them escalating any further. In the investigation we were conducting, this would only happen if there was unfinished business between a person and a spirit connected to them. Here is something we should remember. This investigation was to see if there were spirits within the hotel structure, but it's possible we could pick up on spirits connected to the cottage, or anyone connected to the group, or those observing. We have found a strong connection to Peter's grandfather, but to think he could identify the others we have found would not be likely.

I settled the group down and gave them ten minutes to reconnect with whoever they could. Peter explained to us that the lounge we were sitting in would have originally been living quarters for the White Hart Inn. After what seemed an age I picked up on a Joseph, who seemed to have a strong connection to the pub. Emma got the initial J, associated to the Sarah she had connected to earlier, she thought this was her middle initial, Sarah J. She could now describe what the girl was wearing. She had on a black frock with a white pinny and black boots that laced up at the front. Her hair was in ringlets and she had two bows, one either side. From the look of her Emma said she was in her twenties, but as she explained earlier the girl had a much younger mental age. From where Emma and Ann were sitting, they could see down into the cafe where we had just been. Ann said she could see the grey outline of a group of people, Emma confirmed she could also see them. Jim picked up on the feeling that the group were relieved we had left them alone, so Lewis said he would go back into that room and see what would happen. Ann said she could also see two girls playing in there with a dog. Now, unknown to Ann or Emma, the Dictaphone recorded the voice of a little girl saying, "Hello". I only discovered these, and many more voices when I went through the recording a few days later. I got a real strong connection with someone called Peter, connected to the Peter sitting next to me; I think it was a relative. Ann then got an image of some men sitting smoking clay pipes and playing dominos. She also got a marching band outside the pub in the road. Denis asked if it was a village, or a military band she could see. Ann described the band as wearing red tunics and bearskin helmets, military. Denis could also see a band, but his had white helmets and brown sashes over red tunics. After research the bearskin was only worn by regiments of Guards (as with the other regiments of the Foot Guards). Interestingly the white helmet and red tunic is the dress for the military band of Gibraltar. It was Lewis who asked if there was a connection for the pub to Gibraltar. I know while you are reading these accounts it seems as though things were happening really fast, but in fact there were long periods of inactivity.

It was clear people needed another break, so Vanessa went off to make some tea. Just before we stopped, I said that when we resumed, I wanted each person to ask the spirits to make themselves known. Sometimes when there is clear connection between activity and a specific person, when that person speaks directly to the spirit things can get a little lively.

During the break Peter explained that every name mentioned by the group so far, he could identify and place with people within the pub from around the mid-sixties.

When we resumed it was clear the female members of the group were getting the stronger contacts, so I asked them to ask the spirits to get closer to them. Something then happened that was completely unexpected. Ann could see in her mind's eye a young man hanging from the rafters in the passage just as you come in from the cafe into the lounge. I asked Ann to describe what he was wearing. She described him as having dark hair and wearing a T-shirt, modern looking. She then said he was a bit of a comedian because he was laughing at her and waving. This was a puzzle. Was she seeing a replay of a practical joke?

I asked again for each person in the group to take a turn asking out. Emma went first. Just after she asked out, I saw a shadow go past a small window up in the corner of the room. Both Ann and Emma suddenly felt the temperature drop, as if someone had opened a door. Ann could see a little girl standing just behind Lewis. Lewis was standing behind us to the right of the passage adjoining the lounge to the cafe. Emma confirmed she could see the same thing. The girl then started to walk forward up to the left of Lewis, and Ann described her as waist high to Lewis, with long brown hair, wearing a white pinny and black boots. From what she was wearing Ann put the girl in the Victorian time period. She seemed to have latched herself to Lewis, looking up at him and standing close to him. She stayed with him for some time before fading away.

Ann and Emma could see a group of children down in the cafe, they seemed to be trying to come into the room with us, but something was holding them back. Oddly, Lewis, Ann, Emma, and Peter, suddenly went cold. Peter felt extremely cold, down his back and both arms. He was sitting with me with his back to the group of spirits, as was Lewis. Ann and Emma decided to go and join the spirit children in the cafe. What they didn't know was the children were saying hello to them. I found this out while playing the recording of the evening back later.

As they walked into the cafe, both Ann and Emma were shocked at the temperature drop. Even Lewis commented on it. Considering Peter and I were sitting by the warm fireplace, Peter was actually cold to the touch. Back in the cafe, Ann and Emma were trying out several experiments trying to get the girls to play with them. Jim then asked out, first time he had ever done it. His asking out seemed to have a reaction in the cafe. The temperature dropped even further, almost to the point where you could see your breath. I then started to see the image of an old man standing by Peter. He was small, wearing black baggy trousers that look too big, held up with an old leather belt with an unusual buckle, like an army badge, the round bit in the middle went through a slit in the other end that formed the buckle. He also wore army boots and a white shirt, with the sleeves rolled up. He had a stick, not a walking stick, just a stick he used to carry. I have no idea who it was but it seemed to be connected to Peter in some way, but he wasn't saying. Then a small light flashed in the cafe, moments later Ann and Emma screamed. They had been trying to get a response to knocking and had succeeded. Two taps, then two taps came back. This even surprised Lewis, to the point where he decided to join them. He asked the spirit to do it again and there was a low thud to the right of Emma. All these sounds were recorded as they happened and are on file. Then there was a long period of quiet, so Ann, Emma, and Lewis, all came back into the lounge to explain just what had happened in more detail.

In the picture above are Emma and Ann, explaining to the group what happened in the cafe just a few moments earlier. They reported seeing a room full of children in the cafe. Like a classroom without teachers. Emma went on to explain that the Sarah J she had connected with earlier had learning issues, as do most of the children they had encountered in the cafe. I asked whether it could have been like a Sunday school. Ann thought it possible. Emma said they tried knocking and got a reply, as did Lewis when he asked. As they left to come back into the lounge Emma told the children they would be back to play later and got the names Rachel and Mary. Jim asked them if a car had gone by while they were in the cafe. He was trying to establish the cause of the flash of light he had seen while the girls were in there. Lewis said while down there, two cars had passed by, and yes this could be what Jim had seen, possibly a reflection from the car headlights. I asked Emma and Ann, if they could give us a little more information about the children in the cafe. Emma said, as they walked in there the children gathered around them. There was nobody in charge, in spite of the fact Sarah, the older girl was in there, as Emma had explained earlier, she had learning difficulties and Emma's feelings were she would not be capable of looking after other children.

We would give the lounge another ten minutes then move into the reception hall. Just then I got the mental picture of the old man I had seen earlier, and he had been joined by a black and white sheep dog. Unknown to me, the recorder picked up the sound of a dog barking quite loudly as I told people what I could see. Ann confirmed she could also see the dog. I said the old man looked like a shepherd, a bit like my grandfather. At that point, the old man I could see, shook his head, as if to say, no I'm not. Emma and Ann said from where they were sitting, they could still see the children looking at them and smiling. We would go back in later.

31

We moved into the reception hall, Peter had already told us this was a new addition to the property. It was a long narrow room with a reception counter at one end, but had doors to a conservatory dining room, the lounge, and porch leading to the car park. Our hopes weren't high, but we knew what was there before the building was erected. In this case we believe it was a garden, we may see someone working in the garden from the past, you never know. We could all feel it was warmer in the reception than in the lounge or cafe. I asked out, and immediately Ann could sense the spirit of a vicar. He seemed to be performing a funeral. She saw pews either side of the room and there were lots of people in there listening to the vicar. Remember, this may not be associated to this location, but may be associated with a person within the group. Denis was seeing the same image as Ann. He could also see a lady sitting in the second pew from the front in a large pink brimmed hat, with a bow, and a pink jacket and skirt. Interestingly both Ann and Denis said this lady was the only person in the congregation in colour, all the others were black or grey. We were interrupted and decided to go back into the cafe. I asked Vanessa if they had recently held a wake for someone, but they had not. Emma had an experiment she wanted to test out with the children they had connected to earlier. She had two small ping-pong balls and wanted to see if the children would play with them. We did this first before anyone else tried to contact any other spirit. This would give Emma and Ann a chance to reconnect with the children.

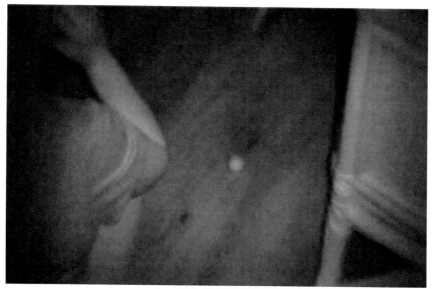

Ann sitting by the ball

Ann had spoken earlier about a little girl she saw sitting under a table in the cafe, so she decided to put a ball on the floor and sit by it close to where the girl was seen. We had all the lights off so Lewis was filming in night vision. Emma was sitting close by and they both placed a ball some feet in front of them and requested the spirit of the children to roll the balls back to them. Emma's ball moved slightly with a rocking motion but apart from that the girls had no luck. I kept getting the image of an old gentleman standing looking at me and smiling, that's all he did, just kept smiling at me.

While they continued trying to get the children to play, I asked the people around the table, (Jim, Denis, Mark, Vanessa, and Peter,) if they were getting any communication at all. Denis said he could see a woman standing in the corner of the room wearing a nurse's uniform. The uniform was blue with a white apron, black stockings, and black shoes. He could not see her face because she was looking out of the window. Jim then heard a tapping sound, as if someone had tapped on a table somewhere in the room. The girls asked whoever it was to repeat the sound. Lewis immediately heard a reply, and it was recorded on the digital recorder. They tried again but this time nothing happened. Ann then asked the children to come and play, instantly I recorded a girl's voice saying hello. I was astonished. Emma and Ann came and sat at our table and we were ready to restart. I asked the group to really concentrate all their efforts to within the cafe. Peter then asked if he could ask out for Fred, if it's the Fred he knew, Peter had something very dear to him in his pocket. Peter asked the spirit of Fred to make himself known to us. The recorder picked up a voice saying, Peter. I instantly saw the old man again, looking at a pocket watch on a chain. He looked down at the watch, and then up at me and smiled. He looked as though he had just done a good day's work, not dressed to the nines but dressed to work. I asked for help from the group to see if they could also see the man. Denis described him better than me. Denis said he had grey hair, with a moustache and was a short chap. His style of clothes was thirties or forties. Emma asked Peter if he recognized who we were picking up on. Peter answered, yes. Peter was doing the correct thing in not giving information away, but letting people concentrate on following their own path with the spirit. Denis also had two other gentlemen standing by the old chap; he thought they could be related. After describing them, Peter said they were the old man's two sons. Our connections then faded. There was a very long silence and I could see some people within the group were looking tired. I decided to end the connection with the spirits and closed the circle down in the correct manner. This makes sure you don't take spirits home with you that have connected with you. But just before we ended, Emma asked Peter who the old man was we were connecting to. Peter explained it was his grandfather. Then Peter reached into his pocket and pulled out a gold pocket watch on a chain saying, this was the item his grandad always wore.

I held the pocket watch Peters grandfather always wore

Sometimes when I give talks to groups people say to me, it's all a load of rubbish. You think so? Most people are fine about ghosts and spirits, as long as they don't have to get involved. As we already know, Peter is interested in the paranormal; this investigation showed him there is something to be discovered. Whether he explores further is his decision, and his alone.

I can now go into the history of the building in depth, and tell you a little more of what I have learnt. At the end of the story you will find a list of landlords and ladies and the years that they held that position. As I said before, part of the Roade House was once a public house known as the White Hart Inn. At the back of this was a cottage. The pub was extremely popular during the 19th and early 20th century. In the following pages you will see photos of the building from 1910, to the present day. Take particular note of the houses to the left of the photos. That area today is a car park. Remember page 22? Denis said he could see a building in the car park.

The white Hart is on the left in the foreground and the Cock is on the right further back. Photo dates from 1910.

© Northamptonshire Archives Service

Two photos of the White Hart Inn from 1924

© Northamptonshire Archives Service

© Northamptonshire Archives Service

One photo from March 1931

39

© Northamptonshire Archives Service

Two photos from 1940

© Northamptonshire Archives Service

The cottage behind the pub 2018

The White Hart Inn.
Today it is the Cafe & Delicatessen part
of Gray's Roade House Hotel. 2018

41

Here is a list of previous Innkeepers of
The White Hart Inn

1885 Joseph Skears
1890 Joseph Skears
1898 Elizabeth Skears (Never opened on a Sunday.)
1906 Harry Skears
1910 Harry Skears
1914 Harry Skears
1940 Jas. E. Whitlock
We know the pub was thriving up until the mid-1950. From then on information is sketchy. It was reported as virtually derelict in the early 1970's, possibly closing in 1973. Then the pub was converted into a restaurant called The Roadhouse. It was then bought in 1983 by Chris and Sue Kewley. In 1997 they bought and incorporated the adjoining cottage to the pub, and made the place into a ten-bedroom hotel called, The Roade House Hotel.

During the investigation, Emma and Ann both sensed children playing in the part of the building we now know as The White Hart Inn. They said the children seemed to be formed as a classroom group, looked after by an older child. My first instinct was Sunday school, but this was a public house, it didn't fit. However, it was noted that a landlady, Mrs. Skears, didn't open the pub on a Sunday. I hunted newspaper records about the pub at that time but could find nothing. There is so much more work to be done on this story but sadly I have hit a brick wall when it comes to further information. As this investigation concluded Peter and Vanessa put the Hotel up for sale. The history of this location now enters a new era.

In years to come what we did on our little investigation will be researched by others who want to piece together their own story of the building. In fact it's really important to write something down for future generations to find, whether in a book, letter, or time capsule placed in the loft of a building. Someone someday will find it, and read about you.

Time Slip

Here's a chilling tale from Leslie Dodd. Leslie got married in 1986, and a year later decided it would be nice to go somewhere with his wife to celebrate their first anniversary. He picked the Llansantffraed Court hotel near Abergavenny in Wales. The Grade II-listed house built in the Queen Anne style was just the place. Leslie phoned up well in advance, spoke to a lady who took his booking and they were all set. Some months later they set off. There were no problems at all on the roads; it was quite an easy run. They came to the point where you turn off the main road. Leslie said at that point everything changed, the sky became dark and grey and the landscape seemed strange. They both looked at each other in concern and said cynically, this isn't good. They drove on, and sure enough they found the sign for the place a few miles further on. They turned left following the sign. Leslie distinctly remembered driving over a cattle grid. He drove on for a quarter of a mile and found the place.

As they pulled up outside, they both sat and looked at each other saying, what! The house was a semi ruin, there was nobody about and it felt and looked foreboding. Leslie asked his wife, if they were in the right place. He got out for a look around and finally decided to actually go into the building. As he entered, he heard a piano playing in the top corner of what was left of the building. He went in a little further, then stopped, he felt a sudden apprehension, something was definitely not right, so he turned and just walked out. He got back into the car and drove off. They were deeply disappointed but managed to find a pub in one of the nearby villages that did accommodation. They booked in, sat down with some drinks, and got talking to

44

an old chap who seemed to know about the area. He asked why they were there. They explained they had booked to stay at the Courtyard Hotel, and said it wasn't quite what they thought it was going to be. The old chap frowned and said, "You what". Leslie repeated what he had said and the old fella said that place burnt down ten or fifteen years ago, nobody has bothered with it since. Leslie explained that that wasn't possible, he had phoned and spoken to someone, and booked a room there a couple of months ago. The old boy shook his head. Leslie asked him if there was a house somewhere with a similar name, maybe they had the wrong place. The old chap said no, there wasn't anywhere else with that name. Leslie and his wife were puzzled, but simply gave up and left it at that, there was nothing more they could do.

Some years later Leslie had remarried, and during a trip to Wales he and his new wife found themselves in the area. Leslie told her he just wanted to check something out. He drove to the Courtyard Hotel, expecting to see the place ruined, but to his astonishment he found himself looking at a beautiful house. They went in and the ladies on reception obviously thought they were looking for a room. Leslie explained he would like to get to the bottom of a mystery. After he had told them the story the women confirmed there was a fire, in about 1997. That was ten years after Leslie and his first wife were there. Leslie then explained about the piano playing. One of the women pointed into a corner and asked, was it in that corner. Leslie confirmed this. The woman took them into a room in that area. Leslie said this is the area he heard the piano playing coming from. The woman said she didn't know about a piano, but people had reported seeing and hearing things in there. She was as puzzled

45

as Leslie and his wife about the ruins they had seen. Leslie has heard about people reporting time slip, but the fire date didn't match with the events he had experienced.

Now, when I am told a fascinating story like this, my first thought is to look into the history of the location, and in this case it paid off. There was a serious fire around the turn of the 19th century and the roofline and windows seem to have been substantially damaged. It was left like this for some years until the main house was totally re-built in 1912, and was completely restored very recently. What really puzzles me is their visit to the pub, and the conversation they had with that old chap. What period of time had they been transported to? Or did they have a conversation in the pub with a ghost? We may never know the truth. However, stories like this come up from time to time and I have even written about them in previous books.

The Ghosts of Hazelwood Road

Here is another story from Leslie about some strange goings on in Bedford. Leslie was living in a house in Hazelwood Road with his second wife and her three young children. At this point in time Leslie was working for the ambulance service so was used to getting up really early in the morning to start his shift. This particular morning, he was shaving in the bathroom when he heard a voice say hello. He turned around expecting to see one of the children but there was nobody there. He said he was feeling quite brave, so said, ok if you want to talk to me go ahead, but there was no reply. A little while after that they were hearing footsteps on the stairs at night. Leslie's wife was getting a little spooked by this and one particular night the footsteps were happening all the time. The kids were in bed and Leslie said, if it happens again, I'll be off out of this bed so fast I'll catch them, thinking it was the children running about. Sure enough, there on the stairs came the sound of running feet. Quick as a flash Leslie shot out of bed and swung open the bedroom door, but saw nothing. He looked in on the children but they were all fast asleep. A while after this they decided to sell the house, not because of what had happened but simply because they wanted to move. They received a phone call one day from the estate agents who for some reason seemed a little upset with them. The estate agent asked them why they had not been there; Leslie said he didn't know what they were talking about. Apparently, they had an appointment at two pm, to show someone around the house. Neither Leslie, or his wife, had any knowledge of this appointment. Leslie added they had both been out at work at that time anyway. The estate agent said, yes, they knew that, but who was the young chap at the window looking out with the hat on, who wouldn't answer the door to let them in. Leslie said there was nobody in the house during the day, but the estate agent replied, there was, he just stood there looking out, not looking at us, more looking through us. Only then did Leslie's wife pipe up and say, oh yes, I've seen him standing by your side of the bed looking out of the window. Leslie said, thanks for that!

On another occasion, still living at the house, they went to see a clairvoyant who was giving a demonstration of her powers in Bedford. Leslie and his wife watched the performance. Then at the end the clairvoyant said she was available for private readings by appointment. Anyway, they made an appointment to go and see her shortly afterwards. On arriving the first thing the woman said was, is there anything you want to ask me. Leslie answered, well yes there is. Before they could say anything the clairvoyant said, "You want to know who is in the house." Leslie was a bit taken aback by this as they hadn't said anything. The clairvoyant went on to tell them about a young Italian boy who had lived in their house years before them. For some reason the boy hadn't passed on and was still trapped in the house. She went on to tell them to go and buy a teddy bear and place it in the corner of the bedroom. They did this and a couple of nights later they were sitting reading in bed when suddenly the temperature in the room dropped drastically. Leslie's wife rang the clairvoyant who said, without hesitation; he's there now isn't he. Leslie explained they could not see the boy. The clairvoyant said, "Something is about to happen but don't worry." Then the temperature suddenly went back to normal and the clairvoyant said, "He's gone now." She went on to say to Leslie, she was in contact with someone surrounded by smoke who wanted to pass on a message to say, don't worry you did your best. Within seconds Leslie knew who she meant. While he was in the ambulance service, he attended a horrific road traffic accident at Ampt Hill in Bedford, where a car was on its roof with a young man inside who burnt to death in front of him, because he couldn't get near him. Leslie is haunted by it to this day. The clairvoyant said, he is telling you not to beat yourself up about it anymore, there was nothing you could have done and he is at peace.

The Hitchhiker of Stranraer

Leslie's next story was about the time he hired a car on holiday to drive around Scotland. He was out in the wilds near Stranraer. It's a town in Inch, in Dumfries and Galloway, which is southwest Scotland. He saw a young fella thumbing a lift so he stopped to pick him up. He told Leslie about this incredibly difficult journey he had made by coach because his brother was dangerously ill, but the coach didn't travel all the way and it was a long walk. Leslie listened to his story and said, "That's no problem jump in". They chatted about this and that as they drove along. Eventually the chap said "It's the next turn up here on the left", so Leslie pulled in and could see a house down a fairly long track so offered to take him down to the door. The man said, "No that's alright let me out here". He got out and Leslie started to turn the car around, looked in his mirror and the chap had vanished. He got out of the car to look around but there was nobody to be seen. He couldn't have made it to the door of the house it was too far away. He had simply vanished. Puzzled by all this Leslie decided to go up to the house to see if he had actually got there. He knocked at the door and a man answered the door. Leslie apologised for bothering him, and what he was about to say might not make sense but this is what has just happened. Leslie explained the earlier events to the man. The man said it sounds like my brother. Leslie asked if he had made it to the cottage. The man shook his head and said no, he couldn't have, he died three years ago. Leslie just stood there speechless.

Here is the last story from Leslie. He was driving to work one morning to Wellingborough Ambulance Station, on the A45 near the Irchester turn. He was driving along, and there was a person dressed like, as he put it, a Goth, seven to seven and a half feet tall, not walking, more gliding along. Leslie watched the figure for about five seconds, overtook it, and when he looked in his mirror the figure had vanished. Leslie told me other ambulance crews had also encountered figures they couldn't explain, especially in the early hours of the morning.

Over the years I have found this a common fact across the UK. Ghost sightings are more common than you think, and I have interviewed hundreds of people who have encountered these figures. When I do public events people tell me they have never seen a ghost. In reply I say it's likely that you have seen one, you just didn't know what it was at the time. Yes, believe me, they are that common.

Ghosts of the S Bar in Stilton

Now here we have several stories of ghosts that frequent the 'S' Bar, once part of The Angel Inn, in the village of Stilton. Stilton is a village and civil parish in Cambridgeshire, England, about 12 miles north of Huntingdon.

This was one of the strangest stories I have ever covered. Not because of its ghosts, but because of the location. It was my old friend Judy Cooper who set this meeting up, and I'm so glad she did. I trust her judgment, and have done so on many investigations in the past. I would be interested to see what she makes of this location. My wife Denise had also joined us for the interviews. During the investigation interviews, the bar closed, and then reopened under new management. This was a great chance for me to compare the two reports of ghosts and spirits within the old building.

I will start by telling you about the first interview I had with the manager in May 2017. At that time it was called The Stilton Tunnels Inn, and the manager was Roy Bains. I began by asking Roy how long he had been at the Inn. He had lived in the village for thirty-four years, and been the manager at the Inn for seven. He knew the place and its history inside out. The Angel Inn, dating from the early 17th century, was rebuilt as an impressive red brick house in the 18th century. It was badly damaged in a fire in 1923, and at that time it was a three-storey building. In the late sixties, early seventies, there was another fire and the top storey was taken off leaving just the two-storey building you see today. The front of the inn is now an Indian Restaurant. The rear is the Stilton Tunnel Inn / S bar. Roy explained that in its heyday the part of the building we were standing in was an impressive stable complex for the Angel Inn.

Layout of the old Angel Inn

53

Image of Stilton with the Bell on the right and the Angel Inn across the road

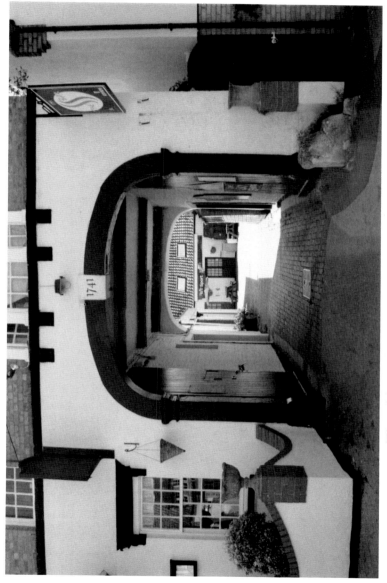

The old coach entrance to the S Bar.

If you look at the modern photo of the entrance to the Inn, on page 55, you will see a doorway to the right as you go through the arch. This door led to part of the Angel that was completely demolished after the fire of 1923. Roy believed the coaching inn stabled up to three hundred horses at a time in its heyday. You can also see two small stone steps in the photo, these were used to help a rather large cheese merchant by the name of Goddard, climb on and off his horse when visiting the pub. Apparently, he paid for steps to be made at every pub he frequented. Cooper Thornhill was innkeeper of the Bell Inn and purchased the Angel Inn in January 1743. It's thought he commissioned several vaults to be built in which to store cheese. Outside the inn a sign was erected which read, Cheese Made in Leicestershire, home of Stilton Cheese. Roy also thinks it was when these vaults were built that they came across the tunnels that run under the streets of Stilton. We will explore these later in the investigation.

Right, now let us go into the ghostly goings on in the pub, and see if they change from before it closes as The Stilton Tunnels Inn, to then reopening as the S bar. First we look at Roy's report and what the locals had seen. Roy believed the activity within the pub picks up after someone goes down into the tunnels, and probably continues for a couple of days afterwards.

Roy said the staff always stacked the beer mats in the centre of the table when tidying up. But when they went in the next morning the mats were placed neatly around the tables. On many occasions when picking up a glass to serve someone, the glass would shatter in their hands before they could pour a drink. Occasionally when members of staff open the fridge door a bottle of drink would fly straight at them. Roy also said the staff leave the cellar light on all day while working in the pub, because it takes so long for it to actually come on. But when they went back down to the cellar the light would be switched off. On one occasion one of the locals, a disabled lad, complained that he couldn't get into the toilet because someone had been in there for ages. Roy went along and knocked on the door, but there was no answer. He knew how to unlock the door from the outside in case of emergencies, but there was nobody in there, and the door was locked from the inside. As Roy spoke, we both saw something move at the end of the bar so we went over to investigate. I knew Judy and Denise were enjoying the location. The atmosphere was electric, and just seemed to cheer you up. Roy and I now stood at the bar. Looking to one side there is a window, the movement we had just seen went across that window. We definitely saw something, but nobody came in. Roy showed me to the front of the property just by the toilets. He explained that at one time this area was part of the cobbled courtyard used by the coaches. He said women using the toilets had often heard people walking, and wheels running as if on cobbles. He added that on Christmas day, women in the toilets washing their hands look up at the mirror and see someone behind them, but when they turn around there would be nobody there. Back in the bar Judy shuddered, as she picked up on spirit activity from past years.

The long narrow bar in the S Bar once a stable block

I explained to Roy that I can often take three years investigating a location, if it's worth investigating then it's worth doing right. Judy decided to wander about to see if she could find a stronger connection to spirit in a different part in the building. Roy took me into what was once the blacksmith and farrier workshop. I asked if people had experienced odd things in there. Roy told me some of the staff, and some customers, had reported being tapped on the shoulder or back. He also said the staff had experienced something strange while down in the cellar. They would hear strange sounds, as if they were not alone, footsteps and shuffling feet. Unfortunately, the cellar and tunnels were flooded at the time we did this interview, so that was off limits, for now at least. In the past Roy has had other mediums visit the pub and told us about a recent one who hesitated at the top of the tunnel steps, saying, there was a strong feeling that was pulling her down into the cellar. Again, the cellar was flooded, but only to the base of the steps. The medium slowly descended into the gloom. At the bottom of the steps she paused, sensing a spirit over to the back of the vaulted room, she said, you're there aren't you. There was a splash in the water as if in reply. She then said, you don't like people down here do you, another splash was heard. The medium then said, you died down here and they never came back for you did they, another splash. The medium then turned and said, "Ok we will leave you in peace" as she climbed back up the steps and returned to the bar.

Now, here is something I had heard about but didn't actually believe. We know the Stilton Tunnel Inn was a stable block at one time, of this there is no doubt. However, some people believe there are identical stables beneath the pub. Various people I have spoken to disbelieve these stories, and to be honest at the time I could see why. I chatted to Roy about coming back to take a good look down the tunnels, and maybe speak to some locals who had experienced strange things within the pub. He agreed to this but the date was left open for when the tunnels were dry enough to get into.

Unfortunately, Roy gave the pub up some months later and the place closed. To say I was disappointed and frustrated would be an understatement, here was an interesting location with ghosts, history, and if true, a unique historical attribute. Undaunted by the closure I was determined to go back one day to find out more about the ghosts and history.

Over a year later I made contact with Kevin Davis, from the Stilton website. Their site is packed with information regarding all aspects of the village and surrounding area. Kevin informed me the Stilton Tunnel Inn had reopened under a new name and management. He kindly passed their contact details on to me and I immediately phoned them. I spoke to Glenn, one of the new managers, and explained what I was doing. I asked if I could go over with a team to record some interviews with locals in the bar, and investigate the tunnels. Glenn agreed to this and a date was set for August 2018. For this investigation I would need the following people. Lewis Dellar, parapsychologist, ex-military and self-confessed tunnel fanatic, Ken Hayes, experienced paranormal investigator with a keen interest in history, Tess Wiltshire, experienced paranormal investigator and Mark Marriot ex-military and has a keen interest in history and the paranormal. This team was ideal for this situation. We needed to go in, record, gather information, and analyse the location in one day. Sounds good, but doesn't always go according to plan.

When we arrived, there were three people in the pub, but Glenn was not there. Terry, the other manager, and his son Nathan were behind the bar. I introduced the team and we were told the tunnels were flooded, to a depth of about eighteen inches. As I wanted to record the ghost stories, the rest of the team decided to investigate the tunnel. We had already planned for the flooding so we were prepared with a change of footwear. Nathan sat with me in the bar and told me the ghost stories he knew about, and some he had experienced first-hand. His own experience came just after they had reopened the pub. At the end of the bar room is a round table with five stools around it.

Every night they place the stools face down on the top of the table, one in the middle with the other four placed around it. Nathan did this one night, and needed to come straight back into the bar about a minute later. The centre stool of the five was standing on the floor with the remaining stools seemingly untouched. Nathan said, to say this was unnerving would be an understatement. People report a cold spot close to the toilets and people see things behind them in the mirrors. Nathan believes the tunnels to be haunted, and again the story of the underground stables came up. He believes some of the spirits emanate from the stable block, supposed to be under the courtyard of the pub. I will get to the bottom of this before the end of the investigation. The ghost stories may also be linked to the fires that destroyed the pub on several occasions.

People gather outside what is left of the Angel Inn 1923

This and the previous photo shows fire damage from 1923. The three firemen in the background are wearing uniforms from that period.

by Marie Kinsay

FIRE completely destroyed a popular local restaurant early today just days after ambitious renovation plans were announced.

Flames engulfed the 236 year-old Georgians Restaurant at Stilton within minutes of the fire starting in an upstairs room.

The roof caved in and carried heavy oak beams through the first floor ceiling into the lounge.

Part of the brick facade collapsed onto the street and the owners fear the rest may have to be demolished.

The blaze started around 2.45 am and the fire brigade received about 16 emergency calls from villagers.

Evacuated

This morning firemen were still on the scene damping down. Part of the High Street has been cordoned off in case the rest of the front collapses.

All the staff had left the building before the fire broke out, but nearby houses were evacuated in case the flames spread.

But the first owner Mr Jack Raynor knew of the tragedy was when he arrived this morning ready to start more work on the roof.

"It was a complete shock," he told the ET. "I don't know what I'm going to do. I started more renovation work only yesterday.

Manager Mr Reg Johnson (31) said a decision to spend another £10-12,000 on the historic building — built in 1741 — had been taken only last week.

"The upstairs was going to be converted into staff quarters and another section was going to be opened as a grill room," he said.

Proprietor, Mr David Cooke has not yet been told of the blaze as he is away.

Firemen spent 2½ hours fighting this morning's blaze at the Georgians Restaurant, Stilton. (Picture by JACK BRINDLEY).

Ian's heartbreak

by Mike Lennox

AMONG spectators at the fire was a man who worked for six months to convert the building into a restaurant.

"It was a bit sickening standing here watching it all go up in 2½ hours",

said Mr Ian Martin (25).

His mother, Mrs Elsie Martin, of 25 High Street, Stilton, took the lease of the building in March last year after it closed as the Concord Club.

"Myself and quite a few local blokes rebuilt it," said Ian. The Georgians

opened in October and the lease was transferred to David and Carole Cooke about Christmas.

A fireman driving a turntable ladder to the blaze said it created a glow in the sky and the flames were visible from Nene Parkway in Peterborough.

Families living in several adjacent homes were evacuated.

Mr Len Payne (55), who lives next door to the restaurant at 6 High Street Stilton, was awakened by a "popping and banging noise" at around 2.30 am.

"I roused the family and we got out," he said. His son, Perkins worker Roy Payne (36), ran to telephone the fire brigade.

The fire of 1977 the building was then called The Georgians Restaurant.

Mark and the rest of the team were having some difficulty down in the cellars tunnels. The water was hampering the search somewhat, and there was a vast quantity of rubble from the previous fires, and from building alterations carried out in the cellars. Undaunted by this the team pressed on carefully. As they continued the water got deeper and the obstacles became unpassable. They reached a point where the tunnel roof came down very low. It was a point where the cellar rooms had been constructed within the tunnel complex and the floor level of the rooms was raised considerably. A blocked up archway leading under the road and towards the public house is where the stable block is thought to be. The problem is the top of the arch is only two feet above the water level and three feet above the new cellar floor. I say new, but it was actually built in the 18th century.

If you look closely you can make out the top of an arch just above the water level. An attempt had been made to drill through the wall, but as you might be able to see, on our visit it was too dangerous to attempt further investigations down there. The following photos will give you an idea of just what the conditions were like for us.

The steps leading down into the first room

The first room had a chequered tile floor. The low arch is to the right.

To the left an archway leads to the next chamber.

This chamber leads onto another that had a small opening at the far end.

Tess and Ken checking through the tunnels

At the end of a chamber we could see the entrance to a tunnel. The water at this point started to get deeper, but Lewis was determined to go further into the tunnels to see what he could find.

This is what greeted him as he crawled through the small gap. After the two fires that the building above suffered, the rubble was thrown down into the tunnel system. Undaunted by this, Lewis crawled through the water, and over the rubble, into the small space you can see in the photo.

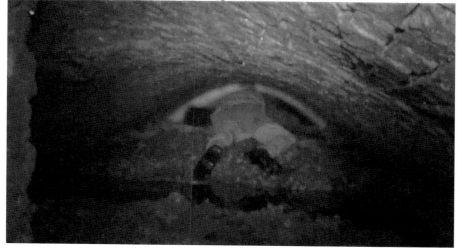

He reported back that the tunnel went on further than he could see with the torch beam, and the rubble seemed to have been pushed back by the force of the flood water. He could also see artefacts relating to the earlier life of the Angel Inn, beer barrels and so on.

Good job Lewis does not suffer from claustrophobia. That was a tight spot.

After the team had dried off and changed their clothes we regrouped and went out to visit the Bell Inn, which is across the road from the S Bar. Could they shed any light on the ghost stories from over the road? Did they have their own ghosts? All they could say was, as far as they knew there were no ghosts in the Bell Inn, and as for the ghosts in the S Bar, they could not say one way or the other. When I asked about the stables underground, they said it was unlikely and impractical. I could see their point of view. Why would you do it with open fields all around? I would love to do an investigation at the Bell Inn, especially after they gave me the history surrounding the place. But that's for another time perhaps.

Back at the S Bar it seems paranormal things occur after people go down into the tunnels. After we left Stilton the S Bar had a flurry of activity. I contacted Nathan again. I needed to satisfy my own curiosity regarding the bricked up tunnel. The hole had been drilled so all I needed to do was put cameras through to see what was on the other side, fingers crossed. A date was set for our return in January 2019. Unfortunately Glenn had left the S Bar so it was just Nathan and his father Terry on hand that day. Something in the back of my mind told me to ring the S Bar before I went back. When I rang them I asked Terry to check the water level in the cellar and to also check if the hole I had seen actually goes right through the wall. On his return Terry said the water level was higher than before and when he put a broom handle into the hole in the wall it didn't go through. Apparently whoever attempted to drill the hole gave up. It's such a shame we will never know what lies behind the blocked arch. Maybe one day an effort will be made to investigate further.

Is the S Bar haunted? Yes I believe it is. But until the flooding is sorted out a full in depth paranormal investigation will have to wait. Will I go back? Yes!

Here is a list of Innkeepers over the years.
1620 / Robert Apreece,
1864 / J. Austin
1885 / Thomas Cox
1898 / John Thos Rayson Coleman
1903 / Frank Horace Coles
1910 / William T Capell

Friendly ghosts in Higham Ferrers

This following story is from a friend of mine, Sue Stow. I met up with her at the Twinwood Aviation Recovery Museum. Sue lives in Higham Ferrers, in a house dating from nineteen thirty-five. She believes the ghost in her house is the lady who lived there before her. The reason for this is Sue is only the second person to live in the property from new. The ghost, Winnie, isn't scary in any way; in fact Sue feels Winnie is quite affectionate and playful. The name Winnie is a girl's name of English origin meaning, "holy peace-making, gentle friend". At the start Sue often saw the image of a lady wearing a lace shawl. Her neighbour opposite confirmed the lady who once lived in the house often wore a shawl.

Then the games started, Sue lost her wristwatch. She searched high and low in all the usual places, but without success. Then almost a year later it showed up under the bed, not at the edges, but right in the centre. Sue explained she looked there when she first lost the watch, there was nothing under there it could have been hidden by, it's a clear space. Now when she loses something in the house she says, come on Winnie, put it back. Sure-enough a couple of days later the item will reappear, not in its original location, but somewhere else. Sue has her places she puts things, but believes Winnie moves them to where she thinks they should be.

One interesting thing occurred one when Sue put some washing on and went to work. She came home to find the washing machine switched off at the plug, the door to it open, and a washing basket in front of the door ready for Sue to take it out.

Before Sue moved into the house, she had it renovated. It's well known that alterations within a property can often release, or heighten, spirit activity. Interestingly while in conversation with neighbours, Sue was told Winnie was a nasty piece of work. Sue is not finding this to be the case, in fact quite the opposite. One day Sue's daughter was getting ready to go out and was sat at Sue's dressing table, when she saw the reflection of a little boy. She said he was about eleven years of age, wearing, what she described as nineteen twenties style clothing, shorts, a tweed jacket, and flat cap.

Sue explained the house has a warm cosy feeling to it. She loves the house and all who dwell within, living or departed. I wish Sue many more happy years in her home, and my thanks for a charming story.

The Ghost Cat from Lancashire

This little story is from Lorraine Horton. Lorraine once lived in an old mill house in Lancashire. They had done alterations to it, as many people do to get a place the way you want it. Lorraine's mother came to live with them and said one day, that's it, I'm not taking that medication anymore. Puzzled by this remark Lorraine asked why. Her mother explained she had been asleep, and woke up to see a cat half way up the wall. Unknown to her mum, during all the renovation work Loraine had done when she first bought the property; they removed a large mantle piece above the fireplace. When Lorraine asked her mum to show her where on the wall the cat was seen, her mum pointed right to the spot where the mantelpiece had been. Other work carried out involved the alteration of the steep staircase, to one with a gentler slope. One day Lorraine saw a cat hovering above the stairs, it then began to walk down and went through the steps below and disappeared. Lorraine could only assume the cat was following the original staircase. I can say right here and now, Lorraine is completely correct in her assumption. Images from the past will follow the route they have always followed, despite anything placed in their path. My thanks to Lorraine for her story.

Mary

Here is a little story from Natalie. When Natalie's parents were looking to buy a house, they went to view a property in Peterborough. The house was old and large, with bags of character, but it was in a disgusting state. There was mould on the walls and ceiling, and had rubbish in most rooms. To say the house was tired would have been an understatement. But for some reason Natalie's mum fell in love with it. It had previously belonged to an elderly couple who had virtually lived in one room. Unable to climb the stairs they were unable to maintain the property so it fell into disrepair. But Natalie's mum could see past the mould and flaking paint and simply fell in love with it.

Twelve years ago, Natalie's uncle Kevin died. He had always lived with Natalie's parents and said if they were to move, he would go with them. Unfortunately, her uncle died before the move to Peterborough. Kevin had loved Christmas, and one Christmas after they had moved into the new house, Natalie was washing up and saw Kevin sitting at the kitchen table, as he used to do. She said he seemed to be enjoying people's conversations. It affected Natalie so much she just burst into tears. She told her mother who she had just seen and her mother said she had also seen him around the house. They still see him from time to time. They also have the ghost of an elderly lady they have named Mary, who helps out from time to time. I say helps out, she is a kind spirit with her own ideas on tidiness. When Natalie was thirteen, she was sitting on the floor in the middle of her bedroom with a friend, when suddenly the wardrobe door opened and some clothes shot out and landed on her. Frightened by this Natalie and her friend ran down stairs and told her mum what had happened. Her mum simply said, well I've been telling you for months to tidy your room and not to just throw your clothes into the wardrobe, if you're not going to listen to me, then maybe you'll listen to Mary. You need to tidy your room now and listen to her. When they returned to the room a picture of Natalie that had been high up on a shelf was lying face down on the floor. From that day on Natalie has always kept her room very tidy, and Mary has left her alone.

The Dormouse of Deanshanger

Here is an investigation that is slightly unusual. The family concerned live in Deanshanger, pronounced deans-hanger, which is a village in South Northamptonshire. Their house was built in the thirties, and is located in a close, at the edge of the village.

In the years I have been studying supernatural activity, I have only come across three cases where an object seems to be haunted. I was asked to investigate the movement of an object that had been the property of the owner's aunt. On her death family members took keepsakes from her property. This particular item was found at the bottom of a wardrobe, under some old coats and handbags. It was in a plastic box, sealed with tape. From the condition of the box and the browning of the tape, I would say it was quite old. On opening the box, the new owner found a rather unusual item. It was a mouse, dressed as a woman in Victorian clothes. On closer examination, the owner found it was in fact a doorstop. A bottle had been half filled with something heavy, and covered in material to form the shape of a mouse, standing in a coat with a basket over one arm. It stood around eighteen inches high, and wore a bonnet and coat, edged with lace frills. It was the strangest looking thing I have seen for quite a while. The owner's family seemed split in their appreciation of the mouse. It was in fact a very good doorstop, if a little creepy.

After using the mouse for a while, the strangest things started to occur. Shuffling sounds, and slight movement of the doorstop. There were two dogs within the property, small terriers, both started to growl and look in the direction of the objects as they moved. These things were unnerving enough but this was nothing compared to what happened next. While sitting watching the TV, the family heard a loud thud, as if something had fallen off a shelf onto the floor. The sound came from the kitchen. On investigation, the doorstop had moved some two feet into the centre of the hallway, leading to the kitchen. It was placed back, and the kitchen was searched but nothing was out of place. The family simply dismissed the incident. Later the same week it happened again. In fact, it carried on happening about twice a week for some time. Arguments about what to do with the doorstop began. Should it be sold, given away, or put into the garden shed. One member of the family really took a liking to the doorstop and persuaded the others it should stay in the house, maybe it would calm down. Interestingly nothing happened within the house when the doorstop was upstairs. But for practical use it was being used in the hallway to prop open the back door when needed. At about Christmas time 2018, while watching TV, the family was shocked to see two pieces of decoration fall from the ceiling. They were some distance apart so it seemed really unusual. As they went to get the foldout steps from the shed, on entering the hallway, there, facing them by the back door stood the mouse, some feet from its original position. Were these incidents connected? They asked me if there was anything I could do. After some thought I decided to put a single night vision camera in the hallway connected to a digital video recorder, and I would leave this running continuously for a week. And guess what, nothing happened that week. I expected to see either of the two dogs moving the mouse, or maybe a real mouse was to blame, but no, nothing at all. Only a day after the camera had been removed the activity started once more. It was time to see if we could find out where this mouse came from. But search as I might I could find nothing. The way the mouse was constructed meant you could not see what the bottle was filled with. This led to speculation that seemed creepy, even by my standards. To this day the mouse stands by the back door, as if watching over the family. One day they will decide what to do with it. This case is ongoing.

I had an update on the mouse doorstop in January 2019. The doorstop was in its original position by the radiator in the hallway. A family member went into the kitchen to make a cup of coffee. As she walked back along the hallway she heard a noise behind her. She froze and called for her daughter to come and see what was happening behind her. Luckily her daughter took this photo of the scene as the lady in the photo was too frightened to look round. Personally, if it's distressing someone in the house that much it's time it went. I would love to take it to a medium friend who could try Psychometry, also known as token-object reading, it's a form of extrasensory perception characterized by the ability to make relevant associations from an object of unknown history by making physical contact with that object. I believe that an object may have an energy field that transfers knowledge regarding that object's history. If that failed I think it should be taken apart and disposed of piece by piece. Don't live with something you fear, get rid of it.

Ghosts of Hawkers Cottage

This eyewitness account came from Colin Evens, of Nether Heyford in Northamptonshire. About forty years ago Colin and his family took a holiday in Coombe, Cornwall. They stayed in Hawkers Cottage. Hawkers Cottages are a pair of stone cob and thatched cottages, named after the famous Vicar of Morwenstow who lived here in the 1820s. In the past Hawkers Cottage was a single house. In the original layout of the building the living accommodation appears to have been on the first floor, whilst the ground floor was occupied by a workshop or perhaps even a byre. By the 1820s the building served as a gentleman's residence and was occupied by writer, poet and the Vicar of Morwenstow, Robert Hawker.

Colin went on to explain the cottage was furnished in the period style and had a thatched roof. Upstairs it had two bedrooms, so he let his two daughters have first choice of the bedrooms. They went into one and didn't like the feeling of it so chose the second one. Colin and his wife had a room with twin beds, and during the night Colin said he woke up to find a black human like shape looking into the mirror that hung on the wall at the foot of the bed. In the gloom he thought it may have been his wife and asked, 'what are you doing standing there'. To his surprise his wife said from the next bed, I thought it was you. Both now wide awake, she too could see the figure. They stared at it for a while, then turned the light on, and there was nothing there. Thankfully when they turned the light off again the figure had gone. However, Colin lay there for a while unable to drop off to sleep again. The window was open and a stream close to the property was making that trickling sound that made Colin want the lavatory. He popped the light on and made his way downstairs, through the cottage, and along the narrow corridor to the toilet, all the time feeling as though he was being followed and watched. Colin said although the place was a little spooky it didn't spoil their holiday. Apparently since their holiday, a TV announcer said on air, that she had spent a short holiday there and had been affected by some type of entity in the cottage. To be honest a property of this age would have the odd ghost or spirit. I would have been surprised if it hadn't.

Ghosts of the Royal Ordnance Depot

This is a location I thought I would never get to write about. In fact it is a place I first visited at the age of six. Back in the sixties the depot was strictly off limits to the general public, and access was only for those who worked there. But at Christmas time in the early sixties, 1963 I believe, the depot hosted a Christmas party for the children from the primary school. I remember the party as if it were yesterday. All the children had a great time, and at the end of the party Father Christmas came in and handed presents to all the boys and girls before they left. Why do I remember it so well? It's probably because I left the party without my present; my memory was awful even then. But joking apart, whenever my mother walked us past the closed gates of the depot, and past the gatehouse portcullis, my imagination would go into overdrive. What was in there that needed guarding so well? The next time I went to the depot I was sixty years old, and just as excited as years before. No, I didn't still believe in Father Christmas, this was my chance to find out what went on behind those closed doors.

I had been told by friends that the depot was now open to the general public, and the new owner was trying to breathe life back into the place by allowing small businesses to move into some of the large buildings. Here is a little bit of history about the depot you should know before we go into the ghost stories.

An ordnance depot at Weedon Bec was authorized by an Act of Parliament in 1803. It was built between 1804 and 1816, and was for the storage of ordnance, to provide a secure inland store for gunpowder, firearms, and other military stores. These could be transported by the nearby Grand Union Canal. The original buildings included eight storehouses, four magazines, and two lodges. Four storehouses were converted to a **barracks,** and two into a military prison. The outbreak of the First World War saw several new storehouses and workshops added to the depot and the prison was closed. The depot was gradually emptied after World War Two and closed in 1965. This is just a simplified history and for its full history I suggest you contact, The Depot Visitors Centre in Weedon Bec.

The Eastern Gatehouse housing the Visitors Centre at Weedon Depot.

This is the exact spot I stood in at the age of six. Now, 54 years later, I get the chance to explore inside the gates that held so many questions for me as a child. Let's take a look inside.

The site is vast. I had no doubt there would be people to interview who had witnessed things they could not explain. As a writer I had been told of a bookshop that traded from here, so that would be my first stop. Each building is numbered, and the bookshop was in building one, shown here on the right in the picture above. I was expecting to find a little shop tucked away somewhere, but how wrong I was. The Booksmiths is a light and comfortable refuge for lovers of books.

They have thousands of books, covering a wide range of topics and genres. While writing this story I would often relax in their coffee lounge and chat with visitors. The shop is on the first floor and links with an art gallery of the same size. The owner of the business, Michael Smith, was the first person to tell me about the ghostly goings on within building one. It was actually in the bookstore where the first strange event happened. Mike was working behind the counter of the coffee bar and moved forward to let someone walk by behind him, when he looked up there was nobody there. He has also experienced phantom customers. He saw what he took to be, a customer, walk towards a window. On enquiring if they needed any help the person had vanished. As you can see in the photo when someone walks to a window they are hidden by the book cases. Michael said this has happened on more than one occasion. In fact it's quite regular.

On another occasion Michael was walking to the back of the store away from the coffee bar, when he noticed a gentleman standing by a window to his right. The man was wearing dark trousers with blue shoes, which Michael said he found rather unusual. On stepping back to talk to the gentleman he could find nobody there, he had vanished into thin air. Other members of staff have also had strange things happen. Lori, who manages the store, has seen books fly from shelves while she is alone, and heard footsteps walking towards her. She explained that while on her own, she felt as though she was constantly being observed. On the ground floor of building one there is a furniture store at one end, and an antique shop at the other. On enquiring in the antique shop if they had seen or heard strange things, they too had experienced a range of events, from hearing footsteps, to seeing a pair of man's legs in white trousers and black knee length boots walking across the shop.

I decided to have a good look around and see what else the site could yield. At that point I was joined by Lewis, Tessie, and Ken. We had decided to do some promotional filming and this location was perfect. Over the years I have found that if you start filming someone in a public location, it sparks interest from people, and filming at Weedon Depot did just that. People started asking us what the filming was about, and before we knew it people were inviting us into other buildings. One such building held the Natural Light Spaces Studio business, run by Tristan Dawson. Tristan told us of a visitor who haunts their studio frequently. It's a figure that walks through a door at one end of the building, walks the full length of the studio to the far window, stands there for a short while as if looking out, then walks back and disappears through the same door, but the image is only seen on infrared cameras. Tristan added, the figure was hazy, but he estimated the height to be between five foot five and five foot seven. He said they have now seen the figure four times over a two week period. Tristan also said he has had visitors in the studio who claim to be psychic, and say they can sense a presence within the room. As far as Tristan is aware his studio room is the only room on the site with a pipe running around it, used for heating during world war two. He believes this may or may not be significant. Lewis did a lap of the studio with an electromagnetic field meter, EMF for short, but found nothing at all. Tristan explained that a couple of guys on site had reported seeing Napoleonic characters walking along the back of the building we were standing in. In fact this sighting had been reported to me before, by others on the site, and it would fit into the route used by soldiers going back to the barracks. Weedon Depot still has secrets to be discovered. One of the original storehouse buildings was converted around 1830 into a military prison. It had one hundred and twenty one cells spread over three floors. A building adjoining this was used as a hospital, and one of the rooms of this was used as a chapel. The chapel also served the military prison. The Garrison Chaplain was William Callendar. During renovations between 1918/1919, a bricked recess in what was then a storeroom was found to contain the font from the former chapel. The font was an exact but miniature replica of the Norman font in Winchester Cathedral, and was subsequently presented to the St Peter's Parish Church in Weedon by the then Commanding Officer.

People have reported hearing singing while walking around the depot towards building seventeen. Could these voices be coming from the old chapel?

Every time I travel to the depot I find new information regarding the ghostly goings on. I doubt it will ever end. All I know is it's a place to be experienced, enjoyed, and protected for future generations.

A Baby Cries

This story comes from Chris Hillyard. Chris is writing a book about the history of Roade Village Rail Cutting with the title, A Cut Above the Rest. He kindly gave me this story from his archives.

On the London North Western Railway, at the village of Ashton in Northamptonshire, early one January morning 1898, George Tew, a Ganger, made a gruesome discovery. As he approached Victoria Bridge, he noticed a brown paper package secured with string, lying close to the down fast main line. Turning the package over with his foot he was shocked to see the hands and lower limbs of a baby boy showing through a tear in the wrapping. He immediately went to the station at Roade to report the circumstances to the station master, Thomas Coxon and PC Avery. The subsequent investigation considered whether the remains were thrown from a train, or from Victoria Bridge itself which was a possible explanation. The coroner asked when the last inspection of the line had been made prior to the discovery of the body. Thomas Coxon stated, it would have been around five thirty the previous evening, and that nineteen trains would have passed on the up pass mainline in the interim prior to the remains being discovered. Having considered the evidence it was concluded at the inquest, it was more likely that the bundle had been placed by the line and had rolled down the embankment. The previous considerations being thought, not possible due to the small amount of damage made to the wrapping and body within, in comparison to what such a method would cause. A local doctor who inspected the body stated that, in his opinion, a case of misadventure during childbirth was the case, and that the poor boy was asphyxiated during birth due to the birth cord being around his neck. The jury's verdict was, found dead, but not how it came by its death. The mother of the new-born was never found. It is said that the cries of the baby could be heard regularly for months after the discovery.

The Twinwood Anniversary Investigation

If you have read Ghost Detective 2 then you will know all about Twinwood Farm. For those who have not read it here is a quick round up of its history.

Twinwood was purpose built by the RAF to train fighter pilots in the skills of night fighting. To intercept bombers and their escort fighters at night, young pilots needed to be able to fly by instrument alone and to recognise enemy planes by their silhouette. Twinwood's other claim to fame is being the last place the American band leader Glenn Miller was seen alive. Miller was due to fly from the United Kingdom to Paris on December 15, 1944, to make arrangements to move his entire band there in the near future. His plane, a single-engine UC-64 Norseman, departed from RAF Twinwood Farm in Clapham, on the outskirts of Bedford, and disappeared while flying over the English Channel. The former RAF Base is now owned and farmed by David and Elizabeth Wooding. They are proud custodians of the former base and hold an annual music festival there every august bank holiday.

I spent two years investigating Twinwood from 2005. In 2015 we decided to do an anniversary investigation to see if anything had changed over the ten year gap. For this to work we would need as many people from the original investigation to be there. Luckily we managed to do just that, with the exception of Andy Ellis who unfortunately couldn't make it. Preparation is everything and this time it would prove a mammoth task. Technology changes rapidly and what was available to us back in 2005 regarding equipment was far from adequate. Our cameras were basic back then and our recording devices were primitive. In 2015 things were very different. My plan was to have two centres of operation during the overnight investigation. One would be in the Aviation Recovery Museum that would also cover the nearby armoury and other buildings. The second operations room would be in the Control Tower. Each team would swap half way through the night. For all this to be monitored throughout the night we would need to lay 200 meters of cable, and use thirteen static infrared cameras, and three mobile infrared cameras, along with five digital and tape recorders. Luckily this time we would have power and heating! It took four hours to set and test the equipment but eventually we were ready to roll.

In the past Twinwood had been alive with ghosts of all kinds, from full body apparitions, to footsteps along empty corridors. Even ghost dogs waking up unsuspecting volunteers spending the night bedded down in one of the sheds. Twinwood had it all. Does it still have it?

The ops room in the tower was set up by Mark Adams, Lorraine and Brian Morris, and Richard Wright. The Museum ops room was set up by Lewis and I, and Robert Allen, with Judy Cooper accessing both as our medium for the evening. People were at liberty to switch ops as they needed to throughout the night.

After all the setup work had been carried out I wanted Lewis to explain what he would be looking for. He was there to study how the team were affected by the surroundings and their reactions to any activity that occurred. He explained that the investigation would not be easy. The team had to try to distance themselves from what they had learnt in the past. Some of them work there voluntarily, so for them it would be especially difficult. Knowing the history of the place there would always be an element of suggestion involved. Lewis is our voice of reason on investigations. That cold spot, the creaking sound, or even the voice heard in the distance, he was there to rationalise these events. He was aware there had been hundreds of reports over the years from unrelated sources regarding recurring phenomena. This really interested him so he was not ruling out the possibility of real activity taking place. Talking to the other members of the team their expectations were high. Richard Wright, our photographer, was looking for a close connection to spirit. I think he had personal reasons for this so this added another element to the night's proceedings. Lorraine and Brian have a close bond to Twinwood. If you spend time up there week after week, year after year the place gets under your skin. Experiencing regular spiritual activity became normal to them. They were calm and I believe comfortable with the expectation of others. I think they wanted people to experience the activity they knew was there. Mark Adams knew the team very well; he knew how they operated and their beliefs. He was a paranormal investigator in his own right so it would be good to see how he approached this night and compare notes. Robert Allen was the founder of the Aviation Recovery Museum at Twinwood and we have known and respected each other for years. His approach for this investigation was practical, but also hopeful it would prove useful to other people. Let me explain this. To Robert, Twinwood and its history is something to be shared. Elizabeth and David Wooding agree with this and promote the location vigorously. People come from all over the world to experience Twinwood's unique atmosphere, but frustratingly it is not given the status it deserves. Despite the efforts of all concerned this little gem in Bedfordshire goes relatively unknown, apart from the annual music festival. So you can see why Robert wants to help people understand its importance. He also believes, as I do, this second investigation will differ greatly from the first. During the first we suffered freezing temperatures and fatigue. But the place was semi derelict and had an air of mystery that was hard to ignore. So let us see what happened this time.

Lewis   Robert

Richard   Judy   Mark

Lorraine   Brian

The first team into the tower were Mark, Lewis, Lorraine, Brian and I. Interestingly it was Lewis who started the ball rolling, he had a name pop into his head of Arnold Westbury. Then Lorraine tried to contact the spirits while in the control tower observation room. She was using the crystal pendulum dowsing method. A crystal pendulum works by tapping into your intuition, or sixth sense. The pendulum acts like a receiver, and transmitter, from your higher guidance, guardian angels or spiritual guide. As the pendulum moves, you gain answers in response to questions – it is best suited to use to answer 'yes' or 'no' questions. Some people describe the way a pendulum works as being like bringing together your rational and intuitive sides.

Lorrain started picking up on a priest she last contacted years ago. Lewis asked for a name but she couldn't remember it. She was in fact picking up on four spirits in the room. The priest was happy that they were honouring the people that were once based there and that our hearts and intentions were good. Mark was drawn to a room along the corridor away from the observations room. He couldn't explain why but on entering the room his EMF, (Electro Magnetic Field) meter gave a reading that suddenly disappeared when he asked out.

Lewis and I went down into the Glenn Miller Museum and left the others to gather as much information as they could in the observation room. What happened next was totally unexpected. Lewis instantly got readings on his EMF meter while standing by the Miller collection, but they were unusual. Little spikes of energy making the meter buzz. I asked for the spirit to do it again and instantly the buzzing sounds came back. Questions were being answered one buzz for yes and two for no. Question, "Had the spirit been there long"? Answer," yes". The questions and answers continued for some time and from them we gleaned that the spirit was female, and worked in the tower in a room upstairs. At two points in the conversation the spirit took over the EMF meter and it just went nuts, as though someone was urgently trying to tell us something. But then the readings came to an abrupt end as though the spirit had left the room.

Lewis in the museum with the EMF meter

Lewis wanted to see if what had just happened was down to a mechanical fault with the meter. He explained in length how the meter worked and how, even unconsciously, it was possible to get the meter to buzz if your grip was wrong. However, we both thought this incident was highly unusual and wish it had continued for longer. Interestingly as our spirit left us the activity upstairs in the observation room picked up. Lewis and I went to the outer room downstairs were the camera monitor was set up. From there we could see all the upper rooms and staircase. At twenty past nine in the evening Brian came down the staircase to join Lewis and me, and reported that he had been knocked to one side by a spirit. Two minutes later we heard footsteps on the staircase and assumed it was Lorraine and Mark coming to join us. As we heard the footsteps we looked at the monitor showing the staircase, but there was nobody there. The hairs on the back of my neck stood up as the footsteps continued. Just then a commotion upstairs caught our attention. Lorraine and Mark came down to tell us what had happened. Lorraine had been shoved in the back as if someone wanted to pass her in a hurry. She said it seemed to come out of the radio room, hit her in the back and continued down the corridor to the staircase. Mark was trying to write things down but his torch dimmed. Lorraine asked if that was the spirit, instantly Mark's torch went off completely. Lorraine asked the spirit to put the torch back on and it did so instantly. Lewis examined Mark's torch and could find nothing wrong with it. Time was against us and we needed to swap locations with the other team.

We decided to meet up in the naffi to have a break.

At this point it was important not to tell the other team what had happened, and as we were about to investigate the Aviation Recovery Museum and other buildings, the other team did the same. Brian, Lorraine, Lewis Mark and I now started our investigation of the Aviation Museum.

After a good look around, Lorraine was drawn to a spot that seemed freezing cold in relation to the rest of the museum. I know Lewis said don't get drawn to cold spots but Lorraine is a good sensitive so it was worth pursuing. We were standing in front of two Mosquito engines. The de Havilland DH.98 Mosquito was a British twin-engine shoulder-winged multi-role combat aircraft, introduced during the Second World War, unusual in that its frame was constructed almost entirely of wood. It was nicknamed The Wooden Wonder or "Mossie to its crews. You need to remember the items in the museum come from crashed planes, and all have a tale to tell. Lorraine was picking up on a strong energy just by these engines so to help her she used her crystal pendulum again. After the usual yes no questions Lorraine was sure the spirit was not connected to the former RAF Twinwood base, but did have a link to the location as it stands today. This may surprise some people. After all we were standing in a place full of WWII items. Let's see how this story unfolds. After more questions it seemed the spirit worked in the building we were standing in, and had very recently passed on to the spirit world. It became apparent the spirit was that of a museum volunteer, and close friend to many at the museum. In life the man had worked on many of the museums exhibits. Unfortunately he had died before finishing his last

renovation job. A bucket with several items of rusty metal in; Brian confirmed the volunteer had been working on these when he died.

The work had been taken over by another member of staff. When Lorraine asked if he was happy with the work being done the answer came back as a positive yes. While Lorraine was talking to the spirit of the old chap, I heard a noise from the far side of the engine display. It was a shuffling and then metal on metal as though something had been moved. Lorraine and Brian explained that the man in question was working on two Mosquito canons that had been excavated from the same crash as the engines, and he was cleaning them up as future display. Lorraine asked me to show her where I had heard the movement while she had been in contact with the spirit. I took her round to the other side of the display and explained what I had heard. There on the floor was a bucket with several items of rusty metal in; Brian confirmed the man had been working on these when he died. Did the metal on metal sound I had heard come from this bucket? It seemed logical to me. Just then we were interrupted by a radio message from the team up at the control tower. They were asking Lewis if the first two internal doors on the ground floor of the tower were closed when we left. We confirmed we had closed them. They informed us the two doors were open when they had entered the tower. It's interesting that each time one team gets paranormal activity in one location the other team get activity at the same time.

Our team decided to move into the long corridor at the end of the museum. The instant we moved into the corridor Mark had a full spike of activity on the EMF meter. All normal lighting was off and we were operating solely on night vision. The various photos you see came from captured frames on the video camera footage; to the normal eye it was pitch black. Mark and Lewis made their way slowly down the long corridor. As they did

Mark started cautiously asking the spirits to join him. As he did so the pendulum Lorraine was holding started to rotate. Marks EMF meter was also showing signs of activity. It made him a little uneasy. Lewis was in logic mode and was looking for natural causes for the meter readings but could find nothing. While this was happening I thought it a good idea to split off from the main group. I wanted to try something back in the Aviation Museum. They have a display cabinet with items from a pilot I had investigated over many years, and I wanted to see if I could contact his spirit. It had been some time since I had been close enough to attempt to contact spirit up at Twinwood. From past experiences I know how problematic this can be. I will not go into too much detail but I was unprepared for the results. As I touched the cabinet it was as if someone had switched on a radio that had several people talking at the same time, each one wanted to know where I had been, it was crazy. I explained I was busy helping other people connect with spirit, and one female spirit voice said firmly, "You haven't finished, you have more to find." I just broke down. In twenty five years of investigating this was the first time. Unknown to me Lewis had slowly walked back to see where I was. He was filming and asked if I was ok. It took me several minutes to compose myself but eventually I said, "Just got told off by some spirits mate." I explained to him about the cabinet and the pilot. I needed to take a break so went to the ops room for a brew. Lewis stayed in the museum trying to make sense of what had just happened. I think from a psychological view point he was interested to find out what had caused such an emotional affect. I just wanted to distance myself from the cabinet. After a short while I was ready to start again. I do not think anybody noticed I had been away. Lewis said as he stood by the cabinet and asked out his torch dipped and flickered. He put it down to coincidence.

Our next target for investigation was the old Armoury Store. It's a building that has proven interesting in the past and one that visitors should always take a look at. Lorraine and Brian took a break so it was just Mark, Lewis, and me. I know Lewis wanted to see what would happen to me in there. I was less keen. For me Twinwood is like opening a door to a room containing all the information you could ever want. The problem is knowing how to shut the door. I asked out again and instantly I knew the female spirit was back but on her own this time. I wanted everyone in this investigation to experience what I was experiencing, so I asked the spirit to make contact with them. I directed her to Judy but the spirit said she was occupied with something else. I asked the spirit if Judy was still in the tower or at another location on the site. I got an instant yes she is in the tower. Lewis got on the radio and asked them to confirm this information and they did. I think for Lewis, and probably Mark, what was happening to me was extremely interesting. But the investigation was set up for others to experience the place. I was happy to take a back seat on this regarding my own abilities. I told Lewis I was stopping this contact and not pursuing it. It was time to regroup and see where people wanted to investigate next.

Robert and I decided to investigate the control tower. We go back many years and when it comes to wanting an honest opinion I trust him. Once in the tower we climbed the staircase to the observation room and settled in, the time was 12.45am. It was so quiet you could hear the owl in the trees next to the tower. We discussed the investigation so far and both came to the same conclusions. When it comes to people's attitudes and approaches to a haunted locations, a lot depends on the condition of the place. Take Twinwood, once a semi derelict place but with a wealth of history, and now it has heating, lighting and services. It has now become a comfortable place to be. It's not scary or sinister and yet the ghost stories continue to be reported, but now somehow it's ok. With nothing happening in the observation room we decided to try downstairs in the Glenn Miller Museum.

Robert Allen standing by the jukebox in the museum

In an attempt to provoke a response we played some forties music while we stood there. I can't explain just how strangely familiar that felt, like being transported back in time. It was really enjoyable. However, it did not trigger any response.

Ok, now how were the others getting on. I was keen to find out about Judy and Richard. I spoke to them back at the Naffi and they remembered some parts of the evening better than others so my main source of information would be the footage they had shot of their investigation. Interestingly it's what they didn't hear that was really interesting about their night. We will come to that later. We start with Robert, Judy, and Richard in the Aviation Recovery Museum. They all reported a strange coldness further down in the museum. Not like a draught, but like curling around you, hugging you. Judy was definitely picking up on a spirit by the name of Walter. He was tall, slim built, and twenty four years old. He was billeted at Twinwood and liked his time there and he survived the war. Judy started to chuckle to herself. When Richard asked what she was getting she explained that Walter said he would have to leave before the others would come to us. Apparently it was the way he said it that made Judy chuckle. She moved a little way down the museum and stopped; she suddenly felt hot and sweaty. She instantly picked up on a jolly man of standard height with a round face and quite stout. He told her he likes a bit of a laugh, but had a military background. Judy said she felt although he put on a face of fun, she felt he hid great sadness in his life. She also felt he had died away from Twinwood, possibly in France. Judy was picking all this up at the spot where I heard the shuffling sound and metal bits knocking together in the bucket but I do not think the two are related.

Moving to the far end of the museum Judy stood by a large rotary engine from a crashed aircraft. She started picking up feelings of dread while standing close to the engine and she felt as though the crew had suffered terrible injuries, horrific was the term she used. At that point power fluctuations started to occur in cameras and torches. Robert said they had been fully charged but the power kept shutting off. Judy then explained how she felt the crew did not die instantly but suffered terribly. She also believed the crash happened in England.

Robert revealed that the plane this engine came from was shot down by a German intruder while landing at RAF Witchword after a mission and the plane burst into flames.

After a pause to reflect Robert, Judy, and Richard decided to go into the long corridor at the end of the museum. As they made their way carefully along the corridor Robert felt a cold shiver go down his neck and back as if someone had blown cold air at him. They were standing at the entrance to the large room containing the street scene and air raid shelter. During the war this room was the commanding officers room. The temperature in there was extremely cold, much colder than the corridor. They decided to sit and see what would happen. They had only been sitting there for two or three minutes when Judy got the strong feeling she needed to be in the quartermaster's store room instead of where they were. Robert led her down the corridor to the room. On entering the room Judy connected with a large stern looking man who shouted and ordered people about. In fact she was quite afraid of him and decided to leave quickly. The three walked to the end of the corridor and to a room on the left that Judy last sat in ten years earlier. The next photo shows the spirit she encountered on that visit.

Would the spirit return this time? Judy sat in the same chair as before and waited to see what would happen.

Robert saw two flashing white lights by the window but on inspection nothing could be found that could have caused them. He then saw something behind Judy but his camera went off before he could take the shot. This happened repeatedly during the night. Judy made contact with a man in uniform, but he had a reddish beret type hat, then the name Martin Spence. She also sensed he was a very private person. Richard then heard a movement in the corridor, but when he looked there was nothing to be seen. To be honest there was so much noise from people talking down the corridor while they took a break Judy had very little chance to really concentrate on her contact. I know Richard wanted to go on a solo session and he got the chance during a little break. He picked a room down the long corridor and settled down for at least fifteen minutes. From the footage he seemed to really be concentrating his efforts toward a particular person. He did not get the responses he wanted so gave up. But unknown to him what he had done influenced the next part of the investigation without him realising it.

After a break Judy, Richard, and Robert walked over to the control tower. It was Richard who wanted to guide this part of the investigation and asked each of them to select a room to sit in. All three of them could hear movement as if people were walking about, and Judy said she could hear a faint conversation close to where she sat in the observation room. Then things got really interesting. Richard started asking if there was anybody there and instantly there came a knocking in reply, but nobody reacted to it. This happened after each question he asked, but again nobody reacted. Then activity was heard downstairs so Richard sat at the top of the stairwell. All three were alone in the tower so who was making the noise downstairs.

This is the corner in the control tower where Glenn Miller sat waiting to board the plane to Paris.

All in all Richard asked out about six times while in the tower and six times he got a reply. As for the movement downstairs, nobody was down there. When they sat downstairs they could hear talking upstairs. It's the classic paranormal conundrum and happens to all who investigate ghosts.

People were now suffering from fatigue so it was time to take down the cameras, roll up the cables and say a fond farewell to my all-time favourite location. The Twinwood ghosts will always be there for those who have the nerve to ask out. Reports of activity come in to me from Twinwood regularly. Even in the daytime you can experience things. That surprises people. It's a fact you are more likely to see a ghost in the daytime than at night.

I hope you have enjoyed the investigations and eyewitness
stories in this book, so until next time
Happy hunting